AIR-ROAD-SEA
ADDLESTONE

THE BLERIOT-WEYMANN-PLESSEY WORKS
1916-1988

By J. H. Rowe

Published by
D. M. & J. L. Barker
47 Sayes Court, Addlestone
Surrey KT15 1NA
Text copyright J. H. Rowe 1992

ISBN 0 9518 658 1 1

THE AUTHOR

James Howard Rowe was born in Wexford, in the south of Ireland, in 1913. During the War he worked in an Admiralty Establishment on radar, after a period in the Irish Electricity Supply Board. Then he moved to Trinity House.

There followed three months in New York, and a time on inertia-sensitive devices at Camberley – mainly Service applications. Then he joined an Aylesbury company on the design of Marine Radar. This company re-formed at Poole, in Dorset, and from there he went to Plessey Radar at Cowes, moving later to its display group at Addlestone.

After the War he took a science degree at London University. He has lived at Addlestone for twenty-four years, and was married for 56 years.

ACKNOWLEDGEMENTS

Thanks are given to many who have helped and those who have given permission to print. I am indebted to the following organisations:

Plessey plc.
Runnymede Borough Council
Surrey County Council
Chertsey Museum
Elmbridge Museum
Brooklands Museum
Surrey Local Studies Library
Addlestone Library
Weybridge Library
Royal Air Force Museum, Hendon
National Motor Museum, Beaulieu
Science Museum
Historic Commercial Vehicle Society
The Shuttleworth Collection
Royal Automobile Club
The Institution of Mechanical Engineers
Companies Registration Office

Cranfield Institute
Ordnance Survey
The Laird Group
Metro-Cammell Weymann Limited
Brixton Estates Limited
Motor Sport Magazine
IPC Transport Press Ltd.
Shell International Petroleum Co. Ltd.
Key Publishing Ltd.
Classic and Sportscar
Stone & Cox (Publications) Ltd.
British Aerospace plc.
LAT Photographic
London Regional Transport
London Country Bus (South West) Ltd.
London Country Bus Services Ltd.
Musée de l'Aérospace, Le Bourget

Apart from these organisations, people who have helped include Mr. Douglas Steadman, Mr. Keith Barkham, Mr. Dixon, Mr. Basten, Mr. Robertson, Miss Dorey, Mr. Ricketts, Mr. and Mrs. R. Marshall, Mr. and Mrs. H. Marshall all of Weymann's, and Madge Melton, who lived in Edith Cottage; Monsieur Louis Blériot, Mr. J. Bingham, Mrs. Wreford, Mr. Whitehouse, Mr. Stephen Spencer, Mrs. Holloway, Mr. Styan, Mr. Feaver, Mr. Grieve of Plessey; Mr. M. Goodall of Brooklands Museum Trust, Mr. Andrews, late Chief Executive, and Mr. G. Stephens of Runnymede Council, as well as Mr. Paul Larkin, former curator of Chertsey Museum, and Miss Jane Sedge, present curator.

Special thanks are offered to Mr. Froggatt, former Works Manager of Weymann's, Mr. John Janaway of the Surrey Local Studies Library, Mr. Gordon Leith of the R. A. F. Museum, and Mr. Chris Taylor of the Historic Commercial Vehicle Society.

It is important not to forget David and Jocelyn Barker, respectively former Chairman of Addlestone Historical Society and former Curator of Chertsey Museum, and Stan Eaves, President of the Society, with a fund of knowledge of historic Addlestone who, with Mrs. Brenda Holmes, Mr. Barker and Mr. Stephen Spencer, corrected the script, with a final correction by Mrs. Pat Brown, whose help was much appreciated.

FIGURES

Printed by Ian Allan Printing Ltd, Addlestone, Surrey KT15 1HY   *Tel:* 0932 855909

CONTENTS

INTRODUCTION

This is the history, from the beginning until Marconi took over, of the factory complex in Station Road, Addlestone, east of the station.

The building was started in 1916 by Louis Blériot, then at Brooklands, and was added to over the years, by himself and his successors, until the seventies. The styles of the additions were not matched, either with the original or with one another.

The account is divided into three parts: the Blériot period, the Weymann time and Plessey.

Front cover:
Aerial view of the factory in 1950

Back cover:
Aerial view of the factory c. 1985

1. ADDLESTONE

The railway station was built in Addlestone in 1848, and the railway now formed a boundary between the greater part of the town on the west and the land attached to Woburn Park. That part between Weybridge Road and the railway, northward of the Bourne, but south of Station Road, was sold by the Earl of Kilmorey in 1868, and building began on the south side of Station Road. The land north of Station Road, not attached to Woburn Park, was known as Roake's Fields. By the time the survey was made for the Ordnance Survey Map of 1914, Alexandra Road, Victoria Road and Albert Road had been largely built up, and many of the buildings along the south side of Station Road were erected (1). The railway which reached Addlestone in 1848 only went from Weybridge to Chertsey until 1866, when it was extended (71).

Susan Harms says her father, Arthur Harms, opened a grocery shop beside the railway on the south-east side in 1870, two years after the sale (2). This is number 196, now a stationer. Two other shops were built as far as the corner of Alexandra Road. On the north side was the Woburn Park Hotel built in 1884, (given as number 111 in the Rates Books, before 1963 when sites were re-numbered), and one large house – Woburn Lodge, number 113 in the Rates Books. Building was slower along the north side of the road, but the south side grew rapidly (33).

Fig. 1a shows part of the 1914 map. Apart from the Woburn Park Hotel and Woburn Lodge next to it, near the station, there are open fields on the north side of Station Road as far as five small houses at the Woburn Hill end (1).

Mr. L. W. Gray, Chief Executive of the Co-operative Society until February 1969, says that Addlestone retained the character of a village until the Great War. The centre of the town was the High Street, remote from the station. A few shops had been built around the station, but much of the north side of Station Road west of the station was open field, with the Village Hall, later the Plaza Cinema, where Osprey House now stands, between the present Methodist Church and the Health Centre (1988). The south side, again with a few shops near the station, ending at the Station Hotel (now The Crouch Oak), was devoted to rather large houses in private grounds. The only industrial building in Addlestone was a linoleum factory just south of the Bourne close to the end of Alexandra Road, and this had become a leather factory owned by Sunbury Leather in 1904 (30).

Within a short distance are Weybridge, New Haw and Chertsey. The activities of one are not independent of another.

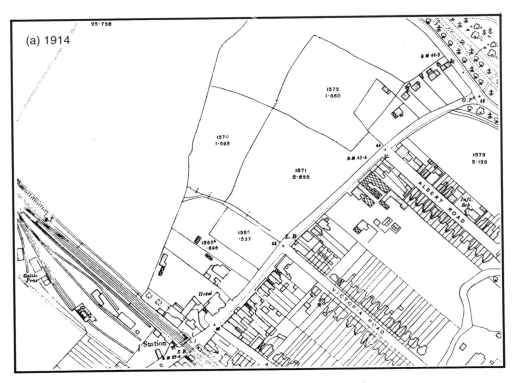

Fig. 1. The factory site as illustrated in local Ordnance Survey maps.

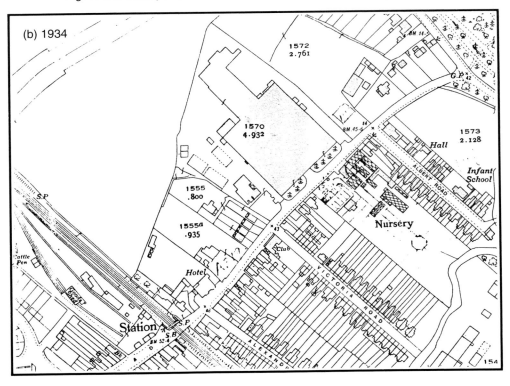

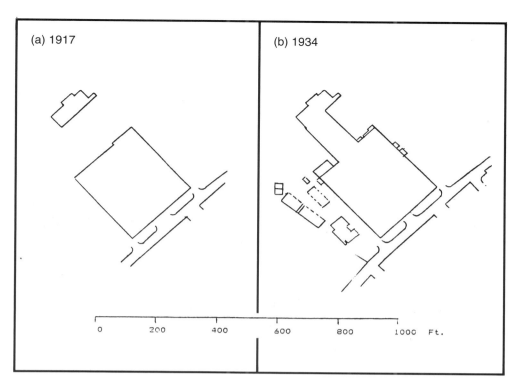

Fig. 2. Building outlines.

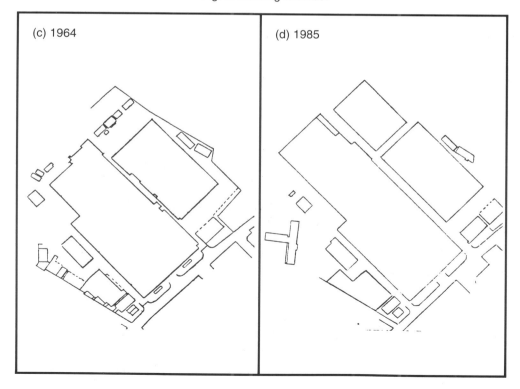

2. BROOKLANDS AND CHANNEL FLIGHT

During the first decade of the century, both cars and aircraft were being developed vigorously. Cars of a sort had already run before 1900, but it was not until 1903 that the Wright brothers first flew. Other machines followed and experiment was considerable. The Wright brothers do not seem to have taken part in this development, but to have used their new machine for demonstration. In 1906/7 a race track and airfield was built at Brooklands by Hugh Fortescue Locke King, clearly with the intention of encouraging progress, at a cost of £150,000. It was in his private estate. The track was 2¾ miles long with a straight finishing section. The curves were steeply banked. Inside the track, sheds and an airfield were built for air experiment, and most of A. V. Roe's early work was done there (31). Fig. 3 shows the clubhouse.

Louis Blériot, Figs. 4 and 6, was born at Cambrai in 1872. He was one of the outstanding figures in the development of aviation, though his early designs rapidly became obsolete. He was a successful maker of car accessories when he became interested in flying. His acetylene car lamp was one of the best (3, 4, 57).

Norbert Chéreau, Figs. 5 and 6, was a graduate of Rennes University: he came to England in 1893 and soon became Blériot's Manager in England (3, 4, 57).

Blériot flew the Channel in 1909. The machine was the result of his eleventh attempt to build a craft that would fly. For that reason it was named Blériot XI. The greatest difficulty seems to have been with engines. The craft had a 3-cylinder Anzani engine rated at 25 horse power, the cylinders being fanwise, on top. It must have been subject to considerable vibration. It also overheated, which led to loss of power. Possibly in an attempt at cooling, a ring of holes was drilled half way down each cylinder, so that the pilot was constantly sprayed with oil. Blériot had no compass when he made the Channel flight, and lost his way in a cloud during the crossing, sighting land again only when he reached Deal, heading towards the Goodwin Sands. He headed back towards Dover. The engine overheated and lost power, but it was saved by a chance shower of rain. He crash-landed on the slopes behind Dover Castle (3, 4, 57). His machine was on display at Selfridges following the flight, and he was well known. But he took orders at once for further building, and did not spend long in demonstration.

The aircraft, enlarged and with a better engine, but otherwise largely unchanged, was built in quantity. Within two months of the Channel crossing he had orders for a hundred aircraft (58). It did training during the War, with some combat duty during the early months. Fig. 7 shows a Blériot XI.

He set up flying schools in France and carried out trials at Issy and Buc. Issy is about 2 km south-south-west of Paris, and Buc about 3 km south of Versailles.

Norbert Chéreau set up a Blériot flying school at Hendon, and another, together with a small factory, at Brooklands in 1913 (32).

He was living in The Hollies in Crockford Park Road, Addlestone, by 1914. He was still there in 1935 and his widow lived in the house in 1944 (22, 33).

About 1914, Louis Blériot gained control of the Deperdussin Aircraft Company after the arrest of Armand Deperdussin for embezzlement and the bankruptcy of the company (32). He purchased land at Addlestone, to be used later.

Fig. 3. Brooklands Clubhouse 1907

Fig. 4. Louis Blériot c. 1914

Fig. 5. Norbert Chéreau c. 1914

Fig. 6. Chéreau and Blériot with car at Brooklands

Fig. 7. Blériot XI at Brooklands

3. PROPELLERS

Aircraft of the first decade of the century had an odd assortment of propellers, some of them no more than paddles fixed to straight members. The design of propellers was rationalised in England by a Weybridge journalist, Arthur Alexander Dashwood Lang (32, 34), Fig. 12. He headed the propeller department of the Bristol & Colonial Aeroplane Co. of Bristol, then went into partnership with David Ernest Garnett early in 1913 to manufacture propellers in Riverside Works, Fig. 9, a building facing the River Thames on the island between the Wey River and the Wey Navigation Canal. The Works Manager was J. D. Titler. There was an office in Piccadilly, London. Riverside Works is no longer there, having been burned down in 1942. Servowarm occupied the site in 1988.

The partnership lasted only months, and a company was registered in the same works in October 1913, with a nominal capital of £4,000, under the directorship of Dashwood Lang, D. W. Monteith and J. H. Stewart Sprott. The War broke out in the following year, and demand for propellers grew, rising from 250 in 1914 to 15,000 by 1918. A large number of aircraft makers was supplied, including the Royal Aircraft Factory, Armstrong-Whitworth, Austin, Beardmore, Boulton & Paul, De Havilland, Graham-White, Martinsyde, Parnall, Sopwith and Vickers. Indeed it seems that Lang became the main supplier of propellers in England. Similarly, one propeller maker became paramount in both France and Germany (32, 34).

As the War progressed, more space was needed. They already had an additional glue shop in Baker Street, Weybridge. They moved to a bigger building in Hamm Moor Lane, seen in Figs. 10 and 11. The building is there still, on the north side of Hamm Moor Lane. It is now (1988) in the hands of Peabody Foods. This view no longer exists, because many other buildings have been erected in what were open fields then. Before the end of the War the premises at Hamm Moor Lane were again not large enough. The Chertsey Drill Hall, belonging to the Territorial Association, was lent to The Lang Propeller Company (34, 36).

Lang, himself, was said to have been interested in amateur theatricals, taking the lead in a performance of "The Dutch Girl" in the Holstein Hall, in Weybridge. A letter in Mr. Goodall's file (34) says that he was called 'Corky' "because of his leg". This suggests that it was artificial.

Propellers were made from Honduras mahogany or walnut planed to ⅞ inches thick and glued together. Then they were smoothly shaped and varnished. Donald Dixon, who lived as a child on the corner of Station Road and Albert Road and watched the erection of the Blériot building, says that offcuts of mahogany were freely available from the Lang Propeller Company, and were used as fire wood. A two-bladed propeller was simple because each layer of wood could extend from one end to the other without a break. But 4-bladed propellers were made for the BE2 aircraft built by the Royal Aircraft Factory. These were supplied at £15 each (32). Fig. 8 shows an 18-foot propeller made for an airship. The Lang Propeller Company also offered a repair service. Propellers were easily damaged (34).

In 1915 T. O. M. Sopwith and Dennis Herbert became directors. In 1917 Lang and Sprott retired (34).

The company closed in 1922, and its work was taken over by The Airscrew Company, newly opened and managed by J. D. Titler in the same building. The Company moved to new buildings across the road and grew, finishing as Airscrew Howden in an extensive complex on the south side of Hamm Moor Lane. It moved, about 1986, to Windmill Road, Sunbury. All the buildings in Hamm Moor Lane were demolished.

Fig. 8. Lang 4-blade propeller at the Riverside Works: "Largest propeller in the world". From left to right: J. D. Titler, Gen. Manager; I. Martin, Inspector; H. Tibbs, Painter; R. Drew, Carpenter; J. Vincent, Carpenter; H. Atkins, Metalworker; W. Bragg, Metalworker; S. Thorne, Chief Inspector

Fig. 9. Riverside Works, Weybridge

Fig. 10. Lang Propeller Co. c. 1916. Front view

Fig. 11. Lang Propeller Co. c. 1916. Side view

Fig. 12. Arthur A. D. Lang

4. THE BLERIOT BUILDING

In summer 1916, the Battle of the Somme began. It made less impact on the Germans than had been hoped. The land effort produced no spectacular gains but enormous slaughter. It merely resulted in stalemate. The new German Albatros played havoc with the older Allied aircraft. The French SPAD 7 appeared soon after. It was superior to earlier craft, and was urgently needed in quantity. Manufacture was undertaken in England as well as in France.

On July 18, 1916, plans for a new factory, to be erected in Station Road, Addlestone, were approved by the Chertsey Council, on submission by L. Blériot (Aeronautics) Ltd., of Brooklands. It was to be built by E. Grace & Son (5, 7 & 8). Motor Sport of Dec., 1963 says "Gaze of Kingston". It was marked boldly "Blériot" and "SPAD", the company to be called "Blériot & Spad Ltd". The article (5), mentioned above, says the costs were met by the Government – £75,000. This is, of course, only a part of the costs outlined in the statement of Louis Blériot to the French Minister of Finance after the War (69). Land, he says, was bought in 1914 and a factory built. He states that his part of the share-holding, of £240,000, was £150,000. It was managed by Norbert Chéreau, as were all Blériot's English enterprises.

Part was built in 1916, and the rest in 1917. The 1916 application (entered in the Approvals Book as "Aeromatic") was for a workshop, wood shed and garage, while that of the following year, July 13, 1917, only mentions an additional workshop, without any other building. No further application was made until 1931. The application again names E. Grace & Son as builder. This leaves the

16

Figs. 13, 14. The Blériot factory under construction 1916

Fig. 15. Aerial view c. 1920

second two-storey building seen in an aerial view, Fig. 15, behind, unaccounted for. But Mr. Norman Froggatt (37) says it was intended as a new town hall for Reading, but was diverted to Addlestone to provide a dope shop! No separate approval has been found, but as the Blériot applications are the first found in the Approvals Book for Station Road, and as those pages were already very tattered, this is not surprising. Previous applications could be missing. The Plessey Site Manager thought this building may have been a previous erection. It does not appear, however, in the 1914 map although it may have been built after 1914, but before 1916. It was used as a hangar in Blériot's time and as a paint store in Weymann's time.

The late Mr. Burgess, whose family owned the bakery on the corner of Station Road and Victoria Road, watched the erection of the original factory. He says the land was very wet, that there were two ponds and a ditch across Roake's Fields. The back of the new factory sank and had to be re-built. Mr. Dixon also says the land was water-logged. Figs. 13 and 14 show the erection in 1916.

One of the original drawings that accompanied the 1916 application was found while the Engineering Department of the Council was being moved from Egham to Addlestone. It is a plan view of the upper floor of the main block, showing that only half of that block was erected in 1916. Certain features are evident. The frontage was much as it is now, about 250 feet, except for minor differences in style. But the depth is only about half that of its later form, seen in Figs. 2a and 15: 151 feet, with both left and right extending beyond. The back wall was thin, suggesting that it was temporary, and that a further extension was to follow. The upper floor was no more than a gallery about 30 feet wide, along the front and both sides. It was not walled off from the centre, but was railed, giving visibility over the main floor. The gallery was only walled in when Plessey took the site over in 1966. The main ground floor was bare except for rows of eight steel uprights every 65 feet holding up the roof.

The drawing shows that, other than part of the front used for offices, the gallery was divided into a wood section, part marked 'Dope', and a large fabric area. Five offices are shown: drawing office, Works Manager, general office, General Manager and, across the stair well, the Board Room.

The bottom of the roof can be seen to be about 20 feet high. The front bay has an ordinary pitched roof, but behind that there are 12 bays of north-light roof, a type not now built. The north-light roof dates from a time when artificial lighting was difficult and dangerous. That part of the roof facing the northern sky was almost vertical and was glazed. The gradual slopes facing the south were unglazed so that the sun could not shine directly on the shop floor.

In July 1917, the second application – mentioned above – was granted to complete the building as outlined in Fig. 2a, almost square. The second two-storey building – already mentioned – behind was used as a hangar for finished aircraft. Fig. 15 is an aerial view of the factory as it was from late 1917 until 1931 (7).

Fig. 2 shows the outline of the premises in 1917, 1934, 1964 and 1985, showing their growth. There is also a plan in 1939, Fig. 28, and another when Plessey took over – Fig. 36 (21).

Fig. 16. S.P.A.D. 7 150 h.p. Hispano Suiza

5. AIRCRAFT BUILT IN ADDLESTONE

Norbert Chéreau, who built and managed the Blériot factory at Brooklands, also managed the Addlestone factory. It is not known when the Brooklands factory closed, though it was still listed in Kelly's Directory as Air Navigation Company in 1922 (22). The last Blériot craft to be built in England seem to have been supplied early in 1916. The Addlestone factory had not been built then, so they must have been made in Brooklands. These craft were obsolete and could no longer be used in combat. They would have been used only as trainers (6).

It was Louis Béchereau of the Deperdussin company, now under Blériot control, who designed the SPAD biplane. It was a new generation of aircraft, far in advance of the old Blériot XI and others. Not only was the aircraft advanced, but it used the new Hispano-Suiza engine, a vast improvement on the old Anzani engine, or on the rotary types that followed. It was a V-eight, water cooled, designed by Marc Birkigt, a Swiss, whom we meet later. The early engine, fitted to the SPAD 7, developed 150 horse power. Later models developed 200 horse power.

The letters S P A D were the initial letters, originally used by Armand Deperdussin, to represent, variously, Société Provisionaire des Aéroplanes Deperdussin, Société Parisienne des Avions Deperdussin and Société des Productions Armand Deperdussin (6, 32). Now the letters stood for Société Anonyme pour Avions et ses Dérives.

SPAD 7 was built at Addlestone. Fig. 16 shows one. It was a tractor single-seat biplane, a fighter. The 150 HP model had a speed of about 120 mph at 2000 metres (6562 feet). The first R.F.C. order for 100 was placed in November 1916. But French drawings were not complete and a sample had to be dismantled for drawing. Performance was poorer than that of French-built models. Those made at Addlestone were nose-heavy and unpopular with pilots. It seems probable that no more than 100 were built at Addlestone. 220 were built in England overall. Blériot is said to have 'signed' aircraft leaving the factory by burning the letter 'B' into the woodwork of seats with a hot iron (6, 27, 28).

Avro 504A, Fig. 17, was also built, a tractor biplane with a 7-cylinder rotary engine of the Gnome type. The seven cylinders of the engine stuck out like the spokes of a wheel, and the whole spun around a fixed crankshaft. The great mass spinning around had a troublesome gyroscopic effect: a turn to right or left caused an upward or downward pressure, depending on the direction of rotation. This must have made piloting both difficult and dangerous. In later engines with cylinders radiating like the spokes of a wheel, called "radial", the practice of a rotating engine was abandoned.

Avro 504A was of 80 to 130 horse power, with engines made by Le Rhône, Clerget or Gnome. The craft was an older design, dating basically from the 1913 504, but with many changes, still used in 1933 and later. Some were used for experimental glider towing in 1940 (38), though with a radial engine. Maximum speed with Le Rhône engine was about 95 mph at sea level, falling to 87 mph at 6,000 feet. It was used mainly as a trainer. A total of 8,340 was built in all English factories, with probably 100 in Addlestone (6, 27, 28).

S.E.5a, Fig. 18, was also built at Addlestone, in the same works. It was an R.A.F. design (Royal Aircraft Factory – now R.A.E.) by H. P. Folland, again using the Hispano-Suiza engine, first 150 HP, later 200 HP. It was a tractor biplane, with speeds between 115 and 132 mph. Between 337 and 360 were built at Addlestone. It was rather later than the SPAD, and probably better in design. It is said to have been the finest fighter of the War (6, 27, 28).

Finished machines were taken, with wings folded, to Brooklands to be flown off.

Fig. 17. Avro 504A

Fig. 18. S.E. 5A

6. AFTER THE GREAT WAR

When the War came to an end in November 1918, the demand for military aircraft collapsed: all aircraft manufacturers, indeed all armament manufacturers, found themselves in difficulty, and Blériot was no exception. Blériot, in England, had not built up any other business of comparable size which might take over.

The aircraft industry had developed largely from war-time needs, and depended for future growth on service requirements, a civil industry having not yet been built. Efforts were made to find an alternative outlet, often in some other direction. Letters written to Blériot show that some sub-contract work was done, and that a Mr. Van Hoytema attempted, unsuccessfully, to form an association with other companies (68). In addition, a cycle-car was designed, to be driven by a motor cycle engine, and attempts were made to find a market in light aircraft.

Blériot was still in control, having the major share-holding, and had clearly made a profit during the War. But taxation was heavy and new markets had to be found. The spirit of co-operation that had made allies during the War was gone. Other constructors had become enemies. He had similar problems in France and also in Italy. The Association of English Aircraft Constructors refused him membership. The problems of the Addlestone factory must have seemed at least as pressing to Norbert Chéreau.

Evidence has not been found that Blériot ever lived in Addlestone, but letters written by Norbert Chéreau (68) in 1919 show that he bought "Riversdale" at Bourne End, and his statement to the French Ministry of Finance (69) says that it cost £2,000, which would have bought a very big house in 1919. A boat house is mentioned as well, and boats. There is also mention of "Le Nid", which we have not been able to identify, with a figure of £6,000 mentioned. That seems too big for a dwelling house and it remains a mystery. The next series of letters is in 1921 and, by that time, the affair is forgotten. It seems curious that, at that time, faced with financial difficulty, he should have bought a large house in England. But probably the end of the War carried a sense of euphoria, and he was not immune.

Blériot must have visited Addlestone. But Norbert Chéreau seems to have been an able manager, and Blériot did not visit much during the War. As we have seen, Chéreau lived in Addlestone, in Crockford Park Road, for over twenty years (22 & 33).

"Flight" of January 3, 1918, reports that the firm was renamed Air Navigation Co. Ltd., as from January 1st, 1918 (38). The company name was later changed to Air Navigation & Engineering Company as from May 20, 1919.

The correspondence of 1919 (68) shows that quotations were received from the Blackburn Company which give an idea of values of the time. These covered 2¾ to 10-horse power motor cycle engines, single and 2-cylinder V, air- and water-cooled, priced from £9-4-9 to £21-2-6. Some of these were for use in the two small cars to be built. The cars have an amateurish quality, such as might have been built in your own garage, and do not compare well with fully engineered models such as Ford Model T, primitive by present standards, but advanced by comparison.

Fig. 19. Blériot Whippet. 1921 racing model seen at Brooklands 1922

Fig. 20. Advertisement: Blériot Whippet

SPECIFICATION
CHAIN DRIVEN MODEL.

ENGINE 8.9 H.P. Blackburne air-cooled twin. 85 mm bore, 88 mm stroke, 998 cc. Detachable cylinder heads ; roller bearing connecting rod big ends ; "Ricardo" aluminium slipper pistons ; side-by-side valves of large diameter, adjustable tappets.

GEAR BOX AND TRANSMISSIONS. All chain 5/8in. × 3/8in. ; chains easily adjustable. Gear box is "Juckes" patent, 3-speed and reverse ; ratios approximate 4 to 1, 7 to 1, 12 to 1. Gear-box together with control mechanism forms one unit and is readily detachable.

ENGINE STARTER. Spring assisted, lever type operated from driver's seat.

CARBURETTER. Zenith single control type, giving 60 miles per gallon.

LUBRICATION. Benton & Stone semi automatic drip feed lubricator with supplementary hand pump.

CLUTCH. "Juckes" patent, Ferodo disc plate, forms integral part of gear box.

CONTROLS. Centrally situated gear and hand-brake levers. Orthodox clutch and brake controls by foot pedals. Single lever throttle control in convenient position behind steering wheel

BRAKES. Interchangeable internal expanding brakes on back axle.

WHEELS. Quickly detachable and interchangeable.

TYRES. 700 × 80 heavy rubber tread.

BODY. Back and seat cushions readily removable exposing commodious lockers.

DIMENSIONS AND WEIGHT.

Wheel Base ..	7ft.
Track	4ft. 2in.
Overall length ...	2ft. 8¼in.
Overall width ...	5ft. 1in.

Weight with standard equipment 8 cwt.

FINISH. Body best "coach finish."

STANDARD EQUIPMENT. Consists of Hood, Screen, Tool Kit, Jack, Pump, Horn, Instruction Booklet, Dynamo Electric Lighting Outfit and Magneto.

SUSPENSION. Quarter Elliptic Springs, back and front

We reserve the right to alter or amend this specification.

𝔗𝔥𝔢 "𝔅𝔩é𝔯𝔦𝔬𝔱 𝔚𝔥𝔦𝔭𝔭𝔢𝔱" 𝔊𝔲𝔞𝔯𝔞𝔫𝔱𝔢𝔢 :

ALL Motor Vehicles and Goods manufactured by the Company carry the following express warranties, which exclude all warranties, conditions, and liabilities whatsoever which might exist as against the Company but for these provisions, viz :—In the event of any defect being disclosed in any motor vehicle or goods, and if the defective part or goods are returned to the Company's Works at Addlestone, carriage paid, within six months after delivery, the Company undertakes to examine same, and should any fault, due to defective material be found on examination by the Company, it will supply, free of charge, the necessary replacements, but the time, labour and other expenditure incurred will in all cases be charged for. The Company's responsibility is limited to the terms of this Guarantee, and it shall not be answerable for any contingent or resulting liability or loss arising through any defect.

THIS GUARANTEE does not relate to defects caused by racing, wear and tear, dirt, misuse, or neglect, or to defects in any Motor, Motor Vehicle, or goods the identification numbers or marks on which have been altered or removed, or which have been let out on hire or which have been sold by any Agent for, or dealer in, Motor Vehicles at less than the full retail prices set out in the Company's price lists current for the time being. The Company also declines responsibility for tyres, ball bearings, speed indicators, extras, or other goods not of its manufacture. All purchasers of Motor Vehicles or Goods from the Company or their Agents shall be deemed to have purchased with notice of these conditions. Prices and specifications are subject to alteration without notice and the retail price will be the price ruling at the time of delivery. Deposits on orders will only be accepted on these conditions.

The word "Agent" is used in a complimentary sense only, and does not imply that the Agent is the legal Agent or representative of the Manufacturers. He has no right to bind the makers or pledge their credit in any way.

Fig. 21. Specification: Blériot Whippet

Fig. 22. Eric Longden light car, Southsea Speed Trials 1922/3

In Addlestone the Blériot Whippet, Figs. 19, 20 and 21 was produced from 1920, and the Eric Longden small car, Fig. 22, from 1922. Both are listed in the 1923/4 motor show catalogues, and Stone & Cox published car specifications (29, 39, 40, 41).

The Blériot Whippet was the Jones-Marchant car, developed in 1919. It was called a 'cycle car', a very light two-seater. All models from 1920 to 1927 were powered by a V-twin motor cycle engine. The first models had a variable-speed belt drive which, both Mr. Dixon and Mr. Burgess say, slipped in the rain. Mr. Burgess adds that the car was high in order that the large pulley on the back axle did not hit the road. Later models had a chain drive and a 3-speed gear box. Synchromesh was, of course, far in the future. It was an open car with a hood as standard. Early models had a kick starter, but a spring-assisted starting handle, operated from the driver's seat, was fitted later. That shown in Fig. 20 seems to be a 1924 model with electric light (39, 40, 41).

In 1920, fifty were lined up and photographed together. The Whippet was priced at £250 to £350 depending on model. The more expensive early models had electric light. Others had a single acetylene motor cycle light complete with generator, as seen in Motor Sport, December 1936. Figs. 20 and 21 show an advertisement and specification. Later the price dropped to £210. It was £170 when a new model came out at £155 in 1923. The price dropped further to £125 later in the year. In 1924 it dropped by another £10 (5).

The Eric Longden company seems to have been in liquidation in 1930. Models were built by the Air Navigation & Engineering Company as late as 1927. 1922 and 1923 models had a V-twin J.A.P. engine, and a Coventry-Simplex 4-cylinder monobloc engine was used later, both with shaft drive. In 1925 there was a starter, but all models had electric light. All were built at Addlestone, and priced at £170 to £210 for the chassis, and £240 to £275 for the complete car. One is pictured in Fig. 22. Numbers are unknown, but by the standard of some cars of that date, both Blériot and Eric Longden cars seem to have been primitive.

In about 1923 the Air Navigation & Engineering Company started on several ultra-light aircraft in the hope of building up new business. A glider had been built in 1922 to George Handasyde's design, and it is believed that A.N.E.C. (Air Navigation & Engineering Company) also built a very light aircraft for him in 1923 (23 & 43). They also built a series under the name A.N.E.C. The designer of the first and second was W. S. Shackleton, whose signature appears in Fig. 23 of A.N.E.C. I in front of the hangar building mentioned in Chapter 4 and seen in the background in Fig. 15.

Only three of A.N.E.C. I were built and one of A.N.E.C. II, which was a little bigger. Both were monoplanes, and had motor cycle engines. A.N.E.C. IV was a biplane, a heavier machine with two seats. It was named "Missel Thrush", and used a 3-cylinder radial engine of 35 and, later, 80 horse power. It is said to have been built in 1926 to the design of John Bewsher (23 & 24). Again, only one was built. Nearly every aircraft builder in the country was trying to sell light aircraft at that time, but engines were not reliable and it was too early for demand to have grown. These attempts did not succeed.

A.N.E.C. III was a heavier machine, built to carry freight or passengers. Three went to Larkin Aircraft Supply Company Ltd. in Melbourne, Australia. It was of 60 feet span and fitted to carry seven passengers, but was later modified to seat eleven. It was called 'hideous'. It had a 350-horse-power Rolls-Royce engine. (24)

All aircraft builders suffered a sudden collapse in business when the War came to an end. But Blériot's factory in England, now The Air Navigation & Engineering Company, went into liquidation in 1927. His report of 1932 to the French Minister of Finance (69) shows that all his property in England, including his house at Bourne End, Riversdale, was sold to pay his debts. He was excluded from membership of the English aircraft trade association and, facing high taxation, was forced into liquidation. The works, which is said to have cost £75,000 to build, was sold to Callender's Cables for £16,000. They failed to open, and sold for £21,000. Finally Weymann took it over in 1928 and opened as Weymann's Motor Bodies (1925) Limited (5, 13, 44).

Louis Blériot died in Paris, probably of heart failure, in 1936 (3, 4, 57).

7. CHARLES TERRES WEYMANN

Charles Terres Weymann lived in Paris and spoke very little English. He was born in 1889 in Port au France, Haiti (some say in 1891 during an Atlantic crossing) (48), (49), (70). His father was American, his mother French. He is shown in Fig. 24, and before the War, when he was experimenting with aircraft, in Fig. 25. He won the 1911 Gordon Bennett air race and took second place in the Schneider Trophy race at Monaco in 1913, both in a Nieuport. He served in the French Air Force during the Great War. He is said to have built his own aircraft. He applied aircraft building principles, especially flexibility, to car body building (49). His flexible body was fabric-covered, the fabric being padded out to a smooth shape. It had a flexible wooden frame, with joints in the frame made from steel plates so that wood never came into contact with wood to rub and make a creaking noise as the frame flexed. This body first emerged in 1921 (44, 45, 46, 49).

He developed and manufactured a range of body fittings and instruments, built bodies and licensed the use of his principles of body building from a factory in Paris. In August 1923 he opened a £1,000 private company in north-west London in association with the brothers, Hermann and Eugen Aron, directors of Rotax Motor Accessories. In November 1925, with the backing of the bank Bernhard, Scholle & Co., he formed Weymann's Motor Bodies (1925) Limited with 55,000 £1 preferred shares and 220,000 one shilling ordinary shares (44). The company bought the premises of the Cunard Motor & Carriage Co. Ltd. in Putney. The site was between Lower Richmond Road and Felsham Road with an entrance in Lower Richmond Road. They set up there under the management of Col. Llewellyn Evans, MIEE, DSO. Lord Montagu joined the board, but resigned in two days. (44)

A company was also opened in Indianapolis in December 1926 but, although Stutz bodies were built by the Weymann method, the fabric body never flourished in America and, by 1926 the fabric body was obsolete in any case (44).

Fig. 23. A.N.E.C. 1, 1923

This may be regarded as Phase 1 of body building development, when the Weymann fabric body was built. In the beginning, bodies had been built by individual coach builders, who had made horse-drawn vehicles. They were based on traditional methods and were quite unsuitable for higher speeds over very rough roads. No thought seems to have been given to flexibility. There was a parallel development, used in America for the mass-produced car, which began with the Ford. It and such makes as Chevrolet were notably noisy.

Fig. 24. Charles Terres Weymann c. 1926

Fig. 25. Weymann in Farmann aircraft 1910/11

8. PUTNEY TO ADDLESTONE

The company moved from Putney to Addlestone in 1928, to the building used by Blériot. O. Heim (46) mentions names from the Putney period, though he includes some who did not join until after the move to Addlestone. He says the General Manager was A. H. Walker who, after a brief period, went to America to set up the Indianapolis company. He mentions E. G. Moreley, Sales Manager, and Frederick C. Webb, the Company Secretary who is seen later, Simpson, the buyer, Lee, the Works Foreman, Brown, Chief Draughtsman, and charge hands Nicholls, Osborne, Pottinger and Bradley. He also speaks of Izod, who did not join until 1929 or 1930 (37), by which time the company had moved to Addlestone. Mr. Norman Froggatt says Sir Henry Seagrave was a director in the early days. He was killed in 1930.

Mr. Norman Froggatt, the son of Arthur Froggatt, has helped a great deal. His careful records are very complete, both of people and of company activities. He joined the company in 1936 as Draughtsman and was subsequently Estimator, Chief Estimator, Assistant Works Manager and, for ten years, Works Manager. He is a Fellow of the Institute of British Carriage and Automobile Manufacturers, having been Chairman of the Southern Centre for three years, and a Judge for the Coachwork Competition at the Motor Show. He is a Liveryman of The Worshipful

Company of Coachmakers and Coach Harness Makers of London, and served on the Councils of The National Federation of Vehicle Traders and the The United Kingdom Joint Wages Board for the vehicle building industry. His name is mentioned frequently.

Among early figures mentioned by several past employees is William Rushton Black who, Mr. Froggatt says, came from Vickers at Crayford, where some buses were built. He joined Weymann's as General Manager, but left in 1934 when Arthur Froggatt came from the Park Royal Company as General Manager. It was, in effect, an exchange, for William Black became General Manager of the Park Royal company. Later he became Chairman of the British Motor Corporation and a life peer. Wooton is remembered by some older employees. He was a mysterious figure. Little seems to be known of him, and rumour is not flattering (37).

Building had not gone beyond the state shown in Fig. 2a, seen in Fig. 15. There was still an open space between the main block and the 2-storey building behind, covered, Mr. Dixon says, with ash. Mr. Dixon worked in Weymann's from about 1931. Fig. 2b shows the state approved by the Council in November, 1931, and in the Ordnance Survey map of 1934 (1, 7). Four bays were built, 90 feet wide and 20 feet high, between the main block and Blériot's hangar, used in Weymann time as a paint store (8).

Mr. Dixon says that just outside the western boundary, behind the group of four houses which are there still, there was a Green Line garage. A garage opened on the Weymann site in October 1930. Mr. Eaves confirms that there was a Green Line garage there in 1931. Later it moved to Addlestone Trading Estate and then to its present site in Station Road. The rate books (33) show that the four houses existed in 1932, but were not mentioned in 1926.

Car bodies were built, at first singly to individual order. Then bodies were built in batches, but never mass-produced. Car body production finally came to an end in 1932 (37). Mr. Dixon mentions the Riley 9. The author saw one of these, new, in 1933 and was impressed by the quality. It is easy to understand why the Weymann body was popular. This must have been among the last. Mr. Froggatt says that bodies were built for the Riley Monaco and the Riley Biarritz, both the Riley 9.

In 1929 the Sports and Social Club was formed. There were then no sports ground, billiards table or tennis court, but the facilities of the Woburn Park Hotel and the Addlestone hard courts, known as 'Scolleys', were used. Sir Henry Seagrave – well known then as the holder of the world land speed record – gave a demonstration of snooker, and a match was won by Jack Henderson of the Maintenance Department over Mr. Black, the General Manager. A little later the tennis section had 48 members including Mr. Webb, Mr. Izod and Mr. Arthur Froggatt, when he joined (13). Although he was not a member of Weymann's staff, Mr. J. D. Titler, once of the Lang Propeller Company and later Managing Director of the Airscrew Company, was on the committee. The club grew, gaining its own billiards room and tennis courts before the War and opening a sports field after the War. The bakery across the road, then in the hands of Mr. Burgess, supplied large quantities of rolls and confectionery.

9. BUSES

Bus bodies started in 1929 with seven that year, reaching almost 1,000 in 1949 (37), though design changed radically. One of the early activities, from 1930 to 1936, was building cabs for lorries. During the First World War, the driver was only protected from the weather by a canvas apron, and this arrangement seems to have lasted long after the War. Other vehicle bodies were also built.

Charles Weymann resigned from the board on 5th January, 1932. The fabric car body was dying by that time and perhaps neither he nor the Berhard, Scholle bank foresaw further development. Bernhard, Scholle & Co. certainly became less interested and the influence of Central Mining & Investment Corporation grew. The 1932 return of directors and share holders (50) shows that their nominee, A. W. Rogers, was now a director, as was Edwin Gilbert Izod, who had been with mining companies in South Africa. A curious coincidence is the presence of Marc Birkigt of Hispano-Suiza among the share-holders. Rolland Jerry (44) says Weymann still lived in France in 1962. (1976 is the date of his death). Mr. Norman Froggatt – the last Works Manager of Weymann's Ltd. – writing in January 1988, has heard that he died in poverty (37). References which mention C. T. Weymann include 44, 45, 46, 47, 48, 49 and 70. After his resignation in 1932, he seems to disappear completely. Very few surviving members of the staff remember him.

The fabric body was obsolete by 1932, and the depression was being felt. It looks as if Charles Weymann was not prepared to face both a radical change in design, and the depression. He seems to have withdrawn from the English venture. He was not a director in 1932, having resigned from the board in January, and only held 200 ordinary shares (44, 50). The number of shares held by all those who gave their address as c/o Bernhard, Scholle were: Preference 8385, Ordinary 9935 (about 15% of preference shares issued, and 4½% of ordinary shares). Lt. Col. Evans was still a director in 1932, and Frederick Webb was still Company Secretary, a position he held until his death in 1949 (13, 37, 50).

The building plan in the schedule of 1939, Fig. 17, shows that, at the outbreak of war, it had both allotments and piggeries. When Edith Cottage, on the east side of the factory building, was acquired in 1937, two hard tennis courts were laid down just behind it. Edith Cottage, gone now, as are those tennis courts, was almost opposite to Albert Road and is seen as the background of Fig. 29 and shown in the 1939 plan, Fig. 28. This plan shows the old paint shop, built in 1935 (37). The tennis courts ceased to exist after the War when the old paint shop, across the drive-way from the main block, was more than doubled in width to form the new paint shop, Fig. 2c.

Edwin Gilbert Izod joined in 1929 or 1930. He was joint Managing Director with Baden R. A. Homfray-Davies when he joined in 1931 and Chairman by 1939, though probably much earlier (37, 50). He came from South Africa, possibly as the nominee of Central Mining & Investment Corporation (13). He joined the Institution of Mechanical Engineers in 1902, worked for Wellams & Robinson at Rugby and joined the Association of Rugby Engineers. In 1911 he went to South

Fig. 26. Weymann staff group 1938

Back row, left to right: Jim Lindon, trim; Jim Knight, finish; George Bannan, polish; Cyril Hutchins, paint; Tom Bradbury, mill; Harry Webster, mount; Cyril Ward, buyer; Ben Carne, inspector; George Hoxley, electrical maintenance; Pop Davies, stock buyer; George Biggs, engineer. Front row: Fred Osborne, panel; Cyril Collins, body; Alf Cousins, General Foreman; F. C. Webb, Company Secretary; E. G. Izod, Managing Director & Chairman; Arthur Froggatt, General Manager; Jack Davies, contract; Harold Cook, Drawing Office; Walter Dodsworth, estimate buyer; R. H. Morter, Assistant General Manager.

Africa, where he worked with two mining companies, one of which may have been The Central Mining & Investment Corporation (52). If we suppose he was 20 in 1902, when he joined the Institution, he would have been 48 in 1930. He died in 1947 (37).

Baden Rhys Aubrey Homfray-Davies came from Park Royal in 1931, becoming Sales Director. He was much concerned in the association with Metropolitan-Cammell, of Birmingham. He left Weymann's in 1955/6 (37). He is described as a man of influence.

Arthur Thomas Froggatt was born in Wellingborough, Northamptonshire, about 1881. He worked on early cars as a coachbuilder and, in 1907, he joined Mulliners in Long Acre, London, and stayed until 1914. It is said that they built aircraft bodies briefly in 1911 (72).

Then he went to Putney until 1923, becoming Works Manager of the Cunard Motor works, before it was bought by Weymann. The Surrey Herald reports three years at Hendon. In 1927 he joined Hall Lewis at Park Royal as General Manager. It was building luxury car bodies, and is said to have built early railcars for the Great Western during that period (37, 72).

In 1934 he moved to Weymann's as General Manager, virtually exchanging positions with William Rushton Black. He was Chairman of Weymann's in 1948, after the death of Izod. He retired on June 30, 1951, and died in July, 1951, at 70 years of age (12, 37). Fig. 27 shows Arthur Froggatt from the cover of Weymag of December 1949.

He was awarded the M.B.E. for his services during the War. He was a Liveryman of the Worshipful Company of Coachmakers and Coach Harness Makers of London, a Fellow and President of the Institute of British Carriage and Automobile Manufacturers and President of the National Federation of Vehicle Trades. He also chaired the Joint Wages Board for the vehicle building industry and, for many years, served on the Panel of Judges for the Coachwork Competition at the Motor Show and was President of Rotarians (37).

Hall Lewis was a South Wales company building and hiring out railway wagons. Its Park Royal works did mainly repairs but, in the 1920s, undertook bus and car body building. In 1931 Hall Lewis collapsed and the Park Royal business was sold to the Yager family as a coachworks. On the death of Harry Yager it was sold to A.E.C. There was a common interest between the Park Royal company and Weymann's. After the War it shared in building the RT3 bus for London Transport. Complete interchangeability was essential. We shall come to RT3 later (37).

These three men – Froggatt, Izod and Homfray-Davies, led Phase 2. They were men of vision and power. All three seem to have been popular and respected. Arthur Froggatt is still well remembered in 1988. They were ready to face change, and clearly saw that change must come. Perhaps they realised that mass production of private cars would eliminate Weymann's methods, even if fabric bodies were not obsolete. They expanded the production of bus bodies and built a smaller number of other bodies – ambulances, lorry bodies and cabs, and prison vans (37). The bus body developed through a composite stage, with wood frame and steel panels. By 1930 the first double-deck type was built and, under Metropolitan-Cammell influence, a metal framed bus followed after 1932 (13).

Metropolitan-Cammell is a Birmingham firm that has been making railway rolling stock for well over 100 years. They had also been building bus bodies for some time, having decided to go into that field in 1929 (12). It was in 1932 that an association between Weymann's and Metropolitan-Cammell (Metcam) led to the formation of a common sales company: Metropolitan-Cammell Weymann, and an agreement to share information and work. Both E. G. Izod and Baden Homfray-Davies were very much involved in this association, as Weymann's had one of the best bus sales organisations and Metcam had long experience, especially in metal-framed bodies. Metropolitan-Cammell Weymann was a non-profit-making company (37). It still exists in the Laird Group.

Fig. 26 shows a group of Weymann staff in 1938 with Edith Cottage behind. Mr. Izod, then Chairman, is in the front row, fifth from the left, with Arthur Froggatt on his left, then Managing Director. On his right side is Mr. F. C. Webb, who was Company Secretary since Putney days (46), and was a member of the Board by 1939 (37). He died in 1949 (13). Mr. Froggatt retired from MCW in 1950 and from Weymann's in June 1951. Mr. Walter Dodsworth was on the Board of Weymann's in 1948 (12, 37). He left in 1956 to join Park Royal Vehicles. In 1938, when the photograph was taken, he was Chief Buyer and Estimator. He is seen sitting, second from the right. Mr. D. J. Davies, then Contracts Manager, on the Board in 1948, is fourth from the right. Between him and Mr. Dodsworth is Mr. Harold Cook, also a Board member in 1948 and later Managing Director (37). Edith Cottage, given as Mr. Izod's address, was used for company entertainment.

The early aerial photograph, Fig. 15, which shows the state at some time between 1917 and 1931, includes the canteen – the building in the left foreground with five windows. No specific approval has been found, but it must have been erected early. The growth of buildings between the original main block and Blériot's hangar, which had started in November 1931, with a narrow linking building (7), was gradual, and took place in several stages until the building between was later increased almost to the width of the main block, though this was not until after the War. Fig. 2b shows the state as seen on the 1934 map. Only a few small buildings have been erected, and they were not in the central block. These were some open sheds, probably for cycles. By March 1939, very little else has been added to the main building, but a new paint shop (later called 'the old paint shop') was erected in 1935 on the east side, across the drive-way (37). This is seen in Fig. 28, shop 4, and was over 300 feet long. War preparations have also been made in the provision of about seventeen separate air raid shelters, a fire station and a decontamination room. Fig. 28 is a ground plan which accompanied a survey of 1939 (25), issued perhaps to raise new stock, perhaps to re-form the company.

This survey, dated March 31, 1939, probably accompanied a fresh prospectus for the issue of new stock mentioned below. The premises, including Edith Cottage, are valued at £64,860, which is below the originally-quoted cost of building Blériot's part (£75,000 (5)), despite considerable additional buildings, piggeries and allotments (25).

Work started on chassis-less bus construction in which the engine, gearbox and other mechanical parts were mounted directly on to the body, as in the present car. Trolley buses were built in this way (9), and, shortly after the War, in conjunction with Leyland, the 'Olympic' appeared (10, 11, 12). The 'Olympic' was a single-deck vehicle taking 40 to 44 passengers.

In 1939 Arthur Froggatt was on the Board, while E. G. Izod was Chairman and Joint Managing Director with B. R. A. Homfray-Davies. Alfred William Rogers, a director of Central Mining & Investment Corporation, was missing. Sir Joseph Napier, described as an underwriting member of Lloyds, was also on the Board. The Central Mining Corporation was not mentioned, though E. G. Izod – giving his address as Edith Cottage – may have represented them. In the 1940 return, the constitution of share capital was changed to 400,000 ordinary shares with a nominal value of 5/- (five shillings) each, of which 398,453 were taken up. It was named Weymann's Motor Bodies (1925) in the returns of 1940. In the returns of 1950 and 1960 it was named Weymann's. (37, 50). The balance of ownership seemed to be changing.

Fig. 27. Arthur Froggatt c. 1949

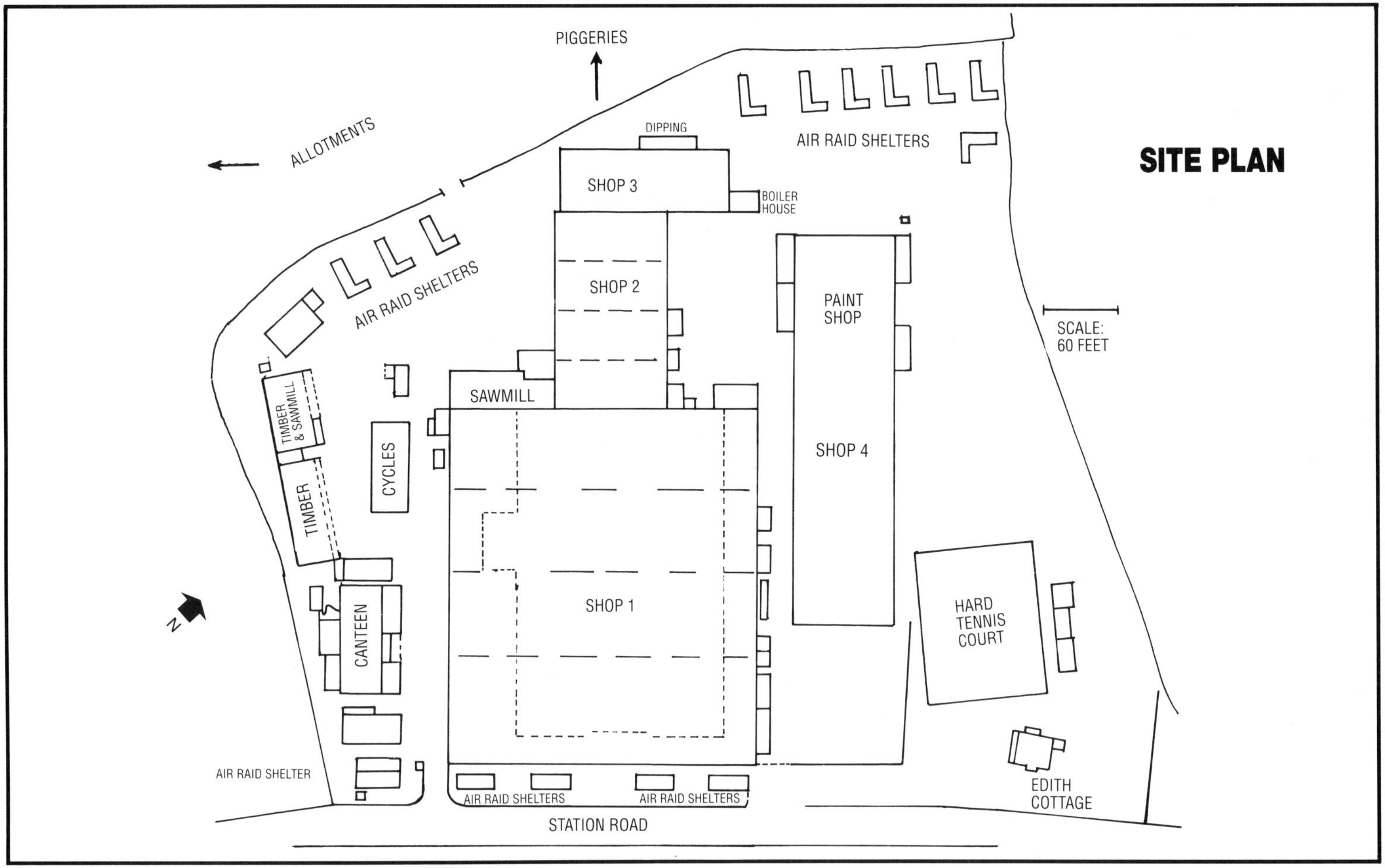

SITE PLAN

SCALE:
60 FEET

PIGGERIES

AIR RAID SHELTERS

ALLOTMENTS

BOILER
HOUSE

DIPPING

SHOP 3

SHOP 2

SHOP 1

SAWMILL

PAINT
SHOP

SHOP 4

HARD
TENNIS
COURT

EDITH
COTTAGE

AIR RAID SHELTERS

AIR RAID SHELTERS

AIR RAID SHELTERS

AIR RAID SHELTERS

STATION ROAD

AIR RAID SHELTER

CYCLES

CANTEEN

TIMBER
& SAWMILL

N

Fig. 28. Building plan 1939

40

10. THE SECOND WORLD WAR AND AFTER

In the Second World War Weymann's built a decreasing number of buses, and many of these were troop carriers. Only the finish differed from peace-time buses. All told, it amounted to 1,521 buses from the beginning of 1939 to the end of 1945. Weymann's also built, in that period, one lorry, one ambulance, five prison vans and 8,804 assorted vehicles for the Ministry of Supply (37). These seem to include armoured vehicles, radio vans, tank transporters, tank chasers, trailers and other vehicles including decompression chambers (12, 13 & 37). The Surrey Herald mentions armour 2½ inches thick, and 6-pounder guns. Some of the work was experimental. There is a verbal mention of tank snorkels tested at Chobham, as well as photographic vans, fire engines, tractors and aircraft parts.

A report, which could refer to any date, tells of the arrival of chassis in large numbers, followed by the departure of finished vehicles, of road tests and mistakes resulting from attempts to drive double-deck buses under the low railway bridge at Hythe in Egham, and another in Walton-on-Thames.

During the War, civilian services were neglected, and there was enormous demand for buses after the War. Authorities and bus lines all over the world needed replacements. Production reached a peak at 972 in 1949, and the number of employees in 1950 was 1500 (13).

One of the best known buses was the RT3, Fig. 29. To build it, J-Block was opened, under the control of Jack Guarnori, in a building in the Weybridge Trading Estate in 1945 (37). The completion of 1,000 RT3s was celebrated in 1950 (13), and, by 1953, 2,400 had been supplied to London Transport (11). RT3 was a double-decker, shown in Figs. 29 and 30. It was built for London Transport in very large numbers and the Park Royal company took part in the production.

Numbers of buses, including RT3, were falling in 1954 when there was redundancy. J-building closed in 1956 (37). A newspaper cutting, unfortunately undated, mentions 40 years of RT service. If production started in 1945, when J-block opened, and sale started in 1946, 40 years of service, mentioned in that cutting, would suggest 1986. The cutting also mentions RF single-deck, used by Green Line.

The chassis-less bus was developed further. 'Olympic' was the first chassis-less bus to be built in quantity. 800 were built by 1953, and over 1000 by 1957 (10, 11). Another of the chassis-less type was the 'Olympian', also a single-deck bus. 'Orion', a double-deck bus weighing less than two tons, appeared in 1952 (11, 12). An assembly works was opened in Port Elizabeth, South Africa. The Works Manager was R. M. Morter, who is seen in Fig. 26, sitting, last on the right. (13)

Fig. 31 is an aerial view of the Addlestone factory in 1950. This was published on the front page of the Silver Jubilee issue of Weymag, the company magazine, for July 1950. It shows the new paint shop, about the same size as the old paint shop, built, Mr. Froggatt says, in 1947. The state is similar to Fig. 2c, though it is 14 years earlier. It does show that, by then, the space between the original main block and the hangar building had been almost filled in. The photograph also shows Edith Cottage, No. 273, now demolished, not shown in Fig. 2, and the chimney of the main boiler house at the end of the hangar building. This building is quite distinct, standing above the rest.

Warleigh, No. 277, is also seen next door. Approval to build it was issued by the Council to Hilda C. Nash in July 1945 (8). Miss Nash was the secretary to the Chairman and also Treasurer to the Sports & Social Club. Later, probably in 1966 when she left Warleigh, she married the postmaster, Mr. Wicks, who lived in Woburn Hill. She died about 1985.

Mr. Izod died in 1947. In 1948 and 1949 Arthur Froggatt was Chairman. All connection with the Central Mining & Investment Company had disappeared, and four directors represented United Molasses, which must have had a controlling interest. They were James Don, J. E. Keable, F. H. Formby and C. G. Allott. Messrs. Homfray-Davies, D. Davies, H. Cook and W. E. Dodsworth were members of the Board. United Molasses was one of the group including Tate & Lyle. In 1949 the Company Secretary was P. H. Gimson. The return of 1950 shows that Mr. Keable was replaced by Mr. McGaw, still of United Molasses. Mr. Izod and Mr. Webb were dead and their dependants had resigned. In 1960 shares were still being acquired by United Molasses. Four directors were still directors of United Molasses. James Don had been replaced by George Walter Scott. The Managing Director was Harold Alfred Cook (37, 50).

In 1963, Weymann's Limited is described as a subsidiary of United Molasses. Production is said to be slowly increasing, but profits were low and production costs high. United Molasses had shipping interests and was clearly having a bad time. Three ships were to be scrapped (19).

From 1950 production fell, not very rapidly, but steadily. In 1960 there were 489 buses, just over half of what were built in 1949. Between 1952 and 1956 a total of 525 vehicle bodies were built for the Ministry of Supply, and between 1958 and 1965, 390 taxi bodies were built for Beardmore. The special body requirements for taxis in London produced a demand for bodies that could not be met by mass production (37).

Mr. Froggatt says the Prudential bought in in Izod's time, and about 1945-6 United Molasses took over. This latter fact is reflected by the figures quoted above as well as in company returns. United Molasses certainly retained control until 1960, and probably later. As post-war demand fell, Leyland bought A.E.C., which then owned the Park Royal company. As a result, work gravitated to Park Royal, as much of it came via Leyland, and away from the M-C W combine.

Harold Cook, seen in the staff group of 1938, Fig. 26, was then Chief Draughtsman. As we have seen, having become Chief Engineer, then joint General Manager, Harold Cook became Managing Director (37).

In 1961 only 289 bus bodies were built, little over half the production of both the year before and that following. This reflects a recession, but may be partly due to the disaster of that year. In what seems to have been a slack period a steel boat was built – Mr. Basten says two boats – not far from the wood-working shop, the 'mill'. Parts were coated with pitch, heated over a gas flame. To save time heating each morning, the flame was kept burning over-night. The pitch boiled over and burst into flame. The fire took hold, and a great deal of damage was done. The woodworking machinery, part-finished buses and part of the main block were destroyed. Fig. 32 shows damage. Buses were burned. Fig. 33 shows the boat (37).

The Surrey Herald suggests a total loss of £500,000 and the loss of 450 jobs (16). However, Mr. Froggatt corrects this figure to £100,000. Inflation has been so high since then that it is hard to evaluate the loss. The Herald says the boat was a 40-ft. cabin cruiser, and that the General Manager then was W. H. Lawrence. He is among the directors of 1966 (37).

Approval was given by the Council for the erection of a temporary replacement building on Aug. 16, 1961, and renewed periodically until the present time. It is shown in Fig. 2c, on the left (west) side of the main building. Plessey called it A5 (7).

Fig. 29. RT3 bus

Fig. 30. Weymann and London Transport group with 1,000th RT3 bus

Fig. 31. Aerial view 1950

45

Fig. 32. Fire damage 1961

Fig. 33. Boat after fire 1961

11. STRIKE AND CLOSURE

In February 1964, a strike broke out in the Finishing Department. It lasted until July – 21 weeks – and involved 85 men. It was caused, so the Herald says, by the inclusion of two union officials of long service among thirteen made redundant. One had 23 years service and the other, 27. As a result, two hundred were reported to be laid off. One hundred and sixty, it is said, left. As in most strikes, feeling was high. Pickets paraded; marches and demonstrations were held. Weymann's said work almost stopped. A combined committee, chaired by A. J. Scamp, Personnel Director of G.E.C., finally arrived at conditions for resumption. The two union officials were to be offered re-employment by Weymann's, provided that they held no union office for three years (17).

The National Union of Vehicle Builders had been active since the beginning but, after several years of inactivity, it suddenly became much more active in Addlestone in 1936. An Addlestone branch was proposed. Discussions were held with Weymann's on rates; the union complained of dilution of labour (54).

The strike caused loss and the fire had been expensive. Some ex-employees think excessive antagonism had grown up between Weymann's management and the National Union of Vehicle Builders, and that the closure was due to conflicting personalities. But Mr. Froggatt's figures show that production had been falling for years, and the purchase of A.E.C. and the Park Royal factory by Leyland, together with the increase in car ownership, must have reduced demand further. Closure was coming, and the strike and fire made it sooner, but did not cause it. The Surrey Herald says production fell to seven buses a week. Seven a week for a whole year would have amounted to 364. In fact, the average over ten years, excluding 1961 and 1964, was 9.82 a week. Seven a week was not many fewer. Certainly the great demand for buses that followed the War had passed. The Herald of June 25th, 1965, reported that Weymann's had been sold to Metropolitan-Cammell two years before, and Mr. Froggatt gives confirmation. The closure was announced in June 1965, to take place early in 1966 (17, 18, 37).

In 1964 the Chairman of Weymann's was Sir Ralph B. Emerson, and the Managing Director, Harold Cook. Mr. Froggatt says both held these positions in 1966. Other directors were D. J. C. Robertson, CBE, AMIEE, MIMechE, and W. A. Scott, CA – apparently not the G. W. Scott mentioned in the 1960 return. The General Manager was W. H. Lawrence and the Company Secretary in 1964 is given as G. E. Lavis (18, 37).

The number of employees remaining in 1965 was 550. In August, 400 employees considered buying the factory from Metropolitan-Cammell, who had already advertised it for sale. It was, however, sold in January 1966, to Brixton Estates, and closed on March 31, 1966 (18, 37).

Mr. Froggatt gives figures of production since 1929. In that period, Weymann's produced 15,104 bus bodies, 337 cars, 65 ambulances, 334 lorry cabs, 102 lorries, 19 prison vans, 9,394 assorted vehicles for the Ministry of Supply and 390 taxi bodies. The total was 25,745 vehicles (37).

It may be noted that Mr. Norman Froggatt is seen in Fig. 30, though any single man is difficult to distinguish. He is standing to the right of Mr. Homfray-Davies and behind him, under the edge of the white placard on the bus. Mr. Davies is standing at the front, in the light-coloured double-breasted suit.

Fig. 34. Detail of fig. 30. Norman Froggatt 5th from left, Baden Rhys Aubrey Homfray-Davies 6th from left

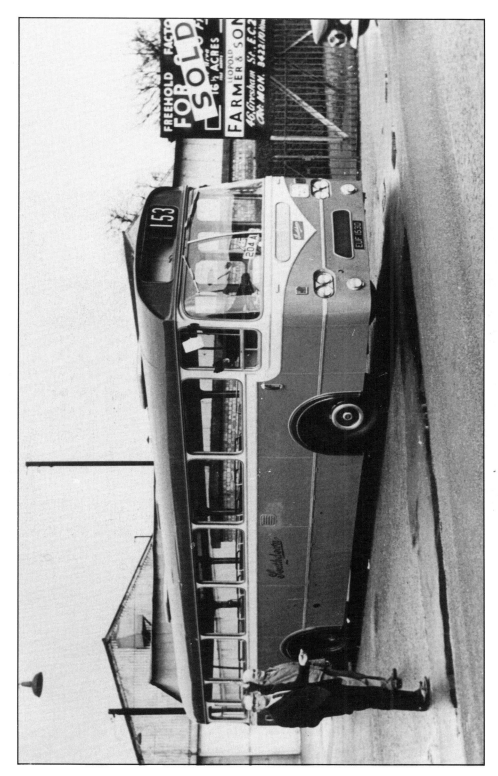

Fig. 35. Last out 1965

12. BRIXTON ESTATES

Throughout 1966, building applications were made by Brixton Estates Ltd. They made thirteen applications to the council, twelve of which were granted (7). The life of the temporary shop that was erected after the fire, called A5 by Plessey, was extended see Fig. 38. The gallery around the inside of Blériot's main block, which lasted throughout Weymann's time, was walled in, forming what were later called the mezzanine floors. The entrance was altered and the frontage re-modelled, but not fundamentally changed. The gable over the entrance was removed. Many of the changes covered by these applications cannot be seen in the outline, as most are internal or changes in style. These changes were evidently agreed with Plessey.

Edith Cottage was demolished in March 1966 (8).

A lease dating from September 1966 for 27 years, was signed by J. Caddey (Coachbuilders) Ltd. for what had been Weymann's New Paint Shop, built in 1947. The part they occupied is shown dotted in Fig. 36 (21). It was called B2 by Plessey. They are remembered by more than one member of Plessey staff from when they first came to Addlestone. An outline is seen in Fig. 38 and is the right-hand half of Fig. 2c. Caddey appears in the directories of 1967 and 1969 at 8, Station Road, Chertsey and 241, Station Road, Addlestone (22). They built commercial bodies of various kinds on a very much smaller scale than Weymann's. The 1969 directory says Caddey moved to Worcestershire in May 1969 (22). Plessey bought the lease from Caddey and leased the rest of the site for 99 years from September 29, 1966, from Brixton Estates, signing the agreement on December 6th, 1966.

13. THE PLESSEY COMPANY

The Plessey Company dates from the First World War. A small company was registered in December 1917 under the managership of W. O. Heyne, a man of German birth, who had spent most of his life in England. It was called Plessey, possibly because his wife came from the Northumberland village of Plessey. But one of the partners was Plessey Parker and that may have had an influence. The registered aims of the company were machine engineering and making pianos, organs and musical instruments. There seems to be some doubt that either pianos or organs were built. Heyne formed other associations (60).

Later capital was injected into what seems to have been a group of associated struggling companies by B. G. Clark, the grandfather of the last Plessey Chairman. His son, the late Alan Clark, entered the business in 1921.

It seems to be on the opening of the British Broadcasting Company in 1922 that Plessey began to forge ahead, first when a contract from Marconi was won by B. G. Clark to make receivers to meet the new demand. That led to the acquisition of premises in Ilford, which were still at the centre of the company when it was taken over. Plessey broadened into the design of its own receivers and the

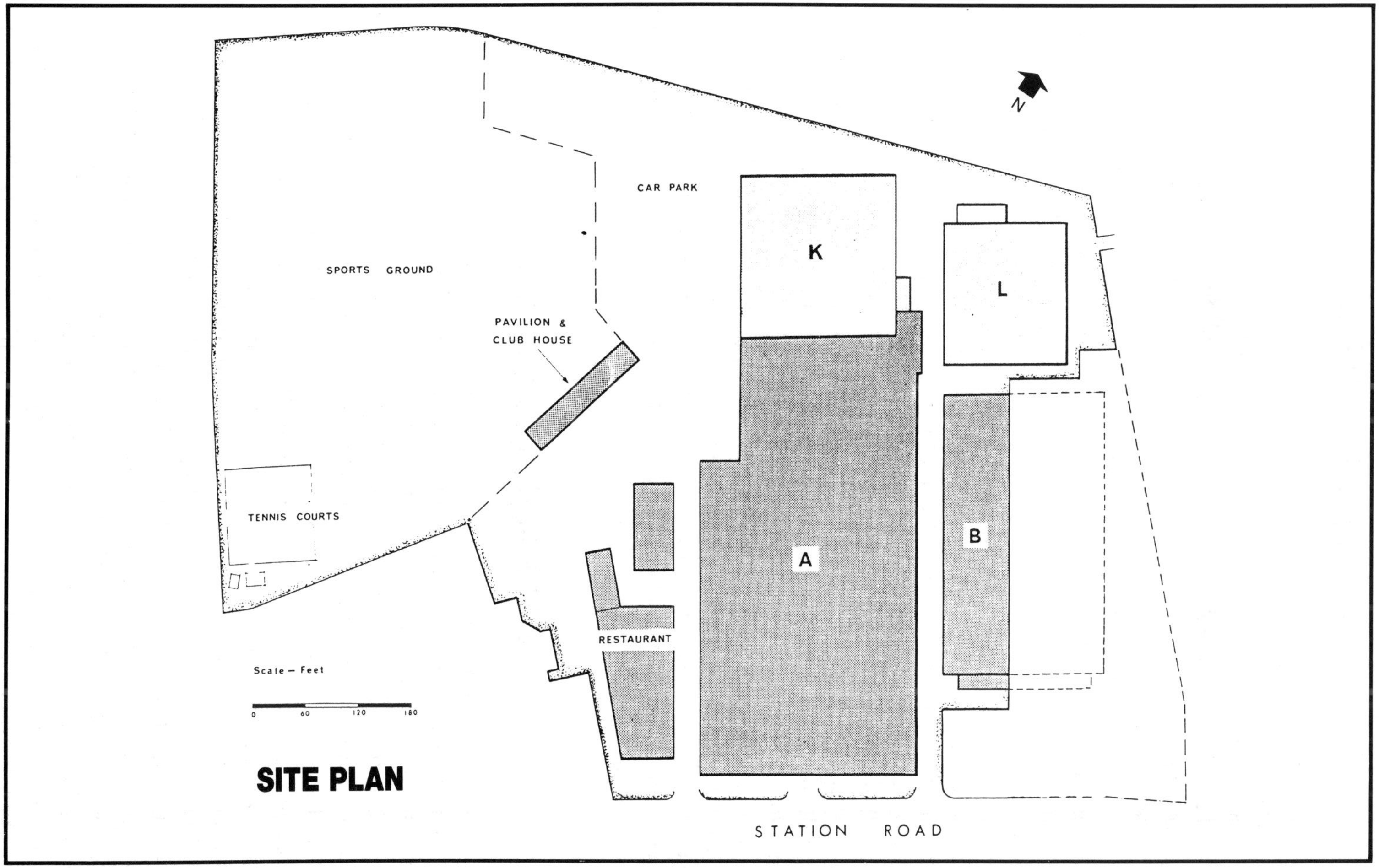

Fig. 36. Plessey site plan

51

manufacture of bells, buzzers, keys (a type of switch) and telephones for the Post Office, as well as cigarette lighters, totalisators, transmitter-receivers and, later, television. Plessey was first a manufacturing company rather than a radio or components company (60).

By 1936/7 turnover exceeded £1 million, and Plessey became a public company in March 1937. A dedicated research centre opened at Caswell near Towcester in 1940. After the War business fell, as it did for many companies, but revived with the Cold War and the Korean War. B. G. Clark died in 1946 and Heyne retired. Alan Clark became Chairman and Managing Director. Business grew rapidly and other companies were acquired, including A.T. & E. and Ericsson, which enlarged the company considerably. Very many other companies followed, often retaining their original names. In 1962 Alan G. Clark died, but the company continued to grow, and spread overseas, becoming international and including many different disciplines (60).

In 1965 the Electronics Group was formed. Existing groups were Telecommunications Group, Components Group and Dynamics Group. Plessey Radar, Plessey Avionics, Communications and Plessey Marine were formed and, soon after, Plessey Defence Systems, as parts of the Electronics Group. In 1976 these became parts of Plessey Electronic Systems Limited – PESL (60, 61).

The Director of the Electronics Group was Group Captain E. Fennessy, who came from the Decca Company. He was largely instrumental in negotiating the transfer of the radar manufacturing undertaking, other than merchant marine radar, from the Decca Company to Plessey Radar Limited. Later he moved to the Post Office.

14. THE MOVE

At first, Plessey Radar occupied the Decca building in Davis Road, Chessington, together with Decca staff. Clearly, the site had to be vacated by Plessey staff as soon as possible. In any case, a date was specified in the agreement of sale. Much work had to be done. Various departments – management, sales, engineering and design, manufacturing, testing, installation and servicing – had to be divided between those joining Plessey and those staying with Decca, and office and shop accommodation had to be prepared and occupied as soon as it was ready.

A building had to be found and suitably converted. This involved building changes, the installation of ventilation and heating systems, false ceilings above which trunking could be concealed, lighting, decorating and furnishing. The conversion was started and much of it completed by Brixton Estates.

Plessey was already a world-wide organisation, and the product would have to be installed and serviced in any part of the world. In many cases, existing establishments could be used. In other cases, buildings had to be found in other countries, and suitably staffed. Sometimes it was possible, at least at first, to share Decca facilities. It was not as though production was just starting, with a demand for local services that would grow slowly. It was already established, and accommodation would be needed very rapidly.

Fig. 37. Frontage 1967

Plessey Radar moved from Chessington to Addlestone early in 1967. The manufacture of transmitters, receivers, aerials and aerial towers, some of them very large, as well as a variety of radar devices, is carried out in a factory near Cowes in a complex of buildings bought from Decca. Sales and overall management went to Addlestone. Displays and display systems were designed, made and tested in Addlestone, and data processing was developed.

The arrival of Plessey Radar in Addlestone was not welcomed. Rail and bus services were not helpful. Local shops had fallen into the practice of closing at lunch time and showed reluctance to accept lunch-time business. This is difficult to understand. It was only about two years since Weymann's closed, with considerable loss of work, and a welcome might have been expected. Of course, requirements were for, at least, manual staff of a different kind, but many who finally joined were, in fact, ex-Weymann people.

Contact was made with councillors and local representatives. Talks were given and conducted tours of the new factory were made. The sports field was made available for local use and to hold the Addlestone Gala. Every effort was made to satisfy local preferences. But it still took several years to overcome opposition.

When Plessey Radar did move to Addlestone, it must be supposed that some still had Decca sympathies and, perhaps, resented the move.

15. PLESSEY RADAR BUILDINGS

The first building application made by Plessey to the council was in March 1967 (7). But although, after that, applications were generally made in the name of Plessey, or Mr. Whitehouse, the Site Manager, on behalf of Plessey, occasional applications were still made by Brixton Estates. Soon after taking over, Plessey built K-Block in line with the main building, just beyond Blériot's old hangar, which had long since been incorporated with the rest, though still visible, as it stands above the rest. K-Block is a single, uniform, three-bay brick building, much bigger than the early additions. It is seen in Fig. 2d, at the end of the main block. Fig. 38 shows the block letters given to the various buildings by Plessey Radar. Staff moved into K-block in July 1969. It was all office space, used by design engineers and draftsmen.

Some time later, L-Block was built behind B-Block, the two Weymann paint shops, and in line with them, across the drive-way from A- and K-Blocks. Again it is seen in Figs. 2d and 38, the building separate from B-block. Some of the design engineers moved in, and a new navigation section was housed.

The north/south part of the pavilion on the left of Fig. 2d, and the car park and playing field, were already in existence. An addition was made to the pavilion a few years ago, perpendicular to the existing part, forming a T-shape.

A drive-way runs around the main building (A- and K-blocks) from a security office inside the gate, at the bottom of Fig. 2, to another gate and security office on the right in Fig. 2. It passes the canteen – the restaurant in Fig. 36 – around the back and between the main block (A-Block and K-Block) and B- and L-Blocks.

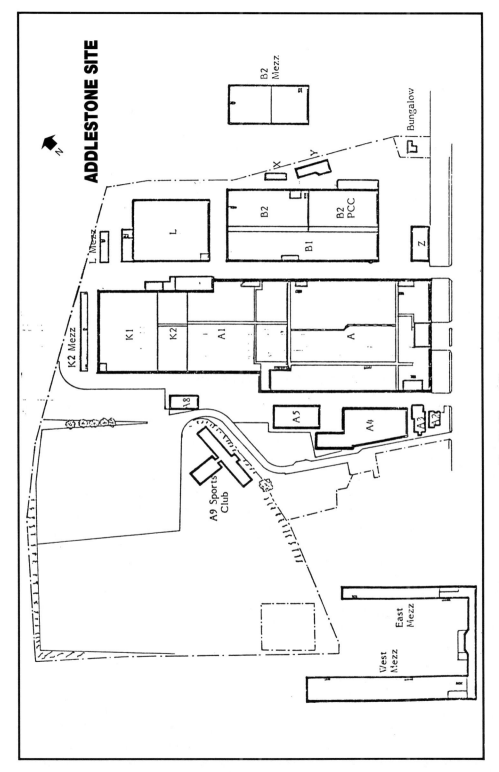

Fig. 38. Plan of Plessey blocks

55

Goods were received at an entrance to A-Block across from B-Block, on the east side. Finished equipments are despatched from the front end of B-Block, Fig. 38. Fig 37 is the front, as in 1967

A general view of one part of the test area is shown in Fig. 39, and a closer view in Fig. 40. The whole test area was much too large to photograph, and broken into several sections. The equipments pictured are display consoles, 12-inch and 16-inch. In both illustrations, the top of a ball is visible, protruding above the table. This so-called "rolling ball" is used to move a symbol to mark any object on the screen, and place a corresponding symbol at the same position of any other display of the family, so that one operator can draw another operator's attention to any feature. The ball moves freely in any direction under the finger of the operator.

Larger units were also made, often mounted with the screen horizontal in the centre of a conference table. Data processing equipment is not shown. Much of it would be seen only as boxes. Data processing equipment operates in various ways, either on radar signals as received, adding additional information obtained from other sources, or compiling a whole artificial display in which each target is reduced to a single symbol, such as a cross.

16. ORGANISATION

As has been said, the management function of Plessey Radar Limited was located at Addlestone. These included market research, sales, pricing, accounting and control of installation and servicing. Heavy equipment was both designed and built at Cowes, while displays and systems of displays were designed, built and tested at Addlestone. This included tabular displays, handling only written data and synthetic information resulting from data processing.

The General Manager of Plessey Radar Limited was W. R. R. Haines, who became Managing Director of the Electronics Group (61). When he left, Mr. Peter Bates became General Manager, probably Managing Director, and, in time, a Group Director, finally moving to the Plessey Board. After Peter Bates, Raymond Wills became General Manager and Managing Director of Plessey Radar.

Plessey was organised into a main Plessey Board with separate groups, each controlled by a separate board. One of these groups was the Electronics Group of which Plessey Radar was a controlled company.

Clem Richards, who was Engineering Manager of Plessey Radar from 1968, eventually became General Manager of Addlestone Region, which included other activities. He later joined Terry Springs at Redditch. The next General Manager of Addlestone Region, Adam Bodnar, is said to have moved later to Marconi/GEC. It was in Bodnar's time that Plessey Displays became separate from Plessey Radar.

Under John Hakes, Plessey Radar moved to a new factory in Chessington in 1984, leaving Plessey Displays behind at Addlestone. A number of the staff had already transferred to an older building in Chessington some years before.

Plessey Electronic Systems Limited (PESL), when it was formed in 1976 (60), was also located at Addlestone. It was formed as the parent company of Plessey

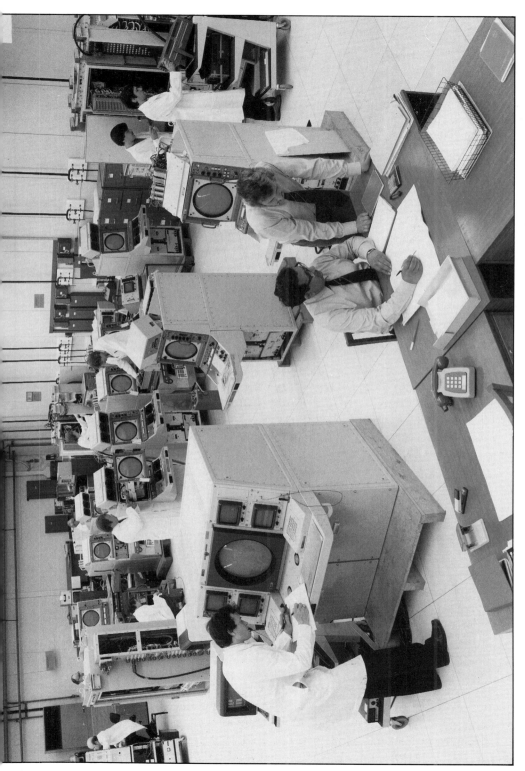

Fig. 39. Test area

Radar, Plessey Airfields, Plessey Marine and, later, Plessey Displays. Alan Jones is remembered as Marine Systems Director, and is listed as a Director of PESL.

Plessey Naval Systems was formed in 1986, when Plessey Marine and Plessey Displays were combined. It was still associated with Addlestone, though controlled from Templecombe. Steven La Pensee was Manager of Command Systems Unit, part of Plessey Naval Systems. (60). As noted below, he became Technical Director of Plessey Displays.

Frank Chorley was Managing Director of Plessey Electronic Systems (PESL), and Alan Jones is said to have been a Director, later on the Plessey Board.

It will be seen that Plessey at Addlestone was a place of constant change. This brought confusion to the staff. It was rumoured that it was part of a plan to avoid tax; that if each company was always new, no corporation tax was due.

17. ACTIVITIES

The earliest units produced in any quantity were Mark 5 displays, confined to 12-inch units: that is, the faces were rather less than 12 inches in diameter. These were designed when transistors were usually of germanium, very sensitive to heat. A policy of offering a wide variety of functions led to a multiplicity of different types.

Later, when silicon transistors were available, with their greater stability and standardisation, a 16-inch standard was adopted as the Mark 8 unit: 12-inch units were confined to naval applications. The conference display was made also, so called because it was larger and had a horizontal face so that people could stand around it. Mark 9 followed as integrated circuits appeared, allowing much more freedom of design.

A computer facility performed data processing. This was widely used in air traffic control and military command systems.

As time went on, the activities of Plessey Radar widened. It was essentially a radar company, making several types of heavy radar. But it was a part of the Plessey Company which was scattered all over the world. Large-scale Air Traffic Control was an important part of its work, but sets were also made for smaller airports, and a variety of wind finding, weather radar and height finders. A small boat radar was also developed, though never manufactured by Plessey.

Associated with these were display systems and families, and command posts for the collection of all battlefield information, land, air and sea, combining radar and tabular displays with additional data, data processing and communications. These command posts had to be easily transportable from place to place.

Although management and planning were, at least in the 70s, located at Addlestone, heavy units were built at Cowes and were never seen at Addlestone, which has always been a display unit, assembling either single displays or groups, and associated equipment.

Displays and systems of displays were designed, built and tested at Addlestone, including tabular displays.

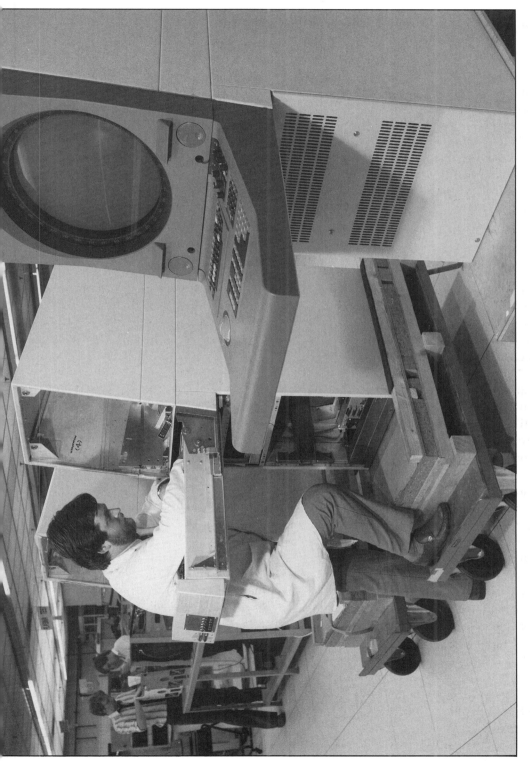

Fig. 40. One part of test area

Air Traffic Control figured largely in the combination of radar and other information from radar heads around the coast and over Europe, so that a complete radar picture of aircraft over western Europe and into the Atlantic could be displayed at one place. Secondary radar information from aircraft is combined, giving details of identity, speed, height, communication frequency, etc. Flight plans are listed. Communication with aircraft and other control centres is included (65).

Perhaps it should be mentioned that, while primary radar relies on reflection from objects, making it possible to locate them, secondary radar excites replying transmitters carried by the target – aircraft or ship – not for location, but to provide information such as its call sign, the frequency of its radio, aircraft height or speed, and even whether a hijacker is on board. A receiver at the radar mast must include equipment to translate the coded messages received into written language to be presented on the display. This translation is one part of data processing.

Data processing, among other things, places this information as written labels beside the radar echoes on a display, following them, and presenting maps of runways, traffic lanes, and other required background. Air traffic control centres may have a hundred or more displays. Corresponding military installations also exist and naval systems form a part.

An essential to data processing is writing of software, that is, writing programmes for computers to enable them to manipulate data or to perform whatever feats are required. A computer is useless without instructions, and a programme is only a series of instructions. Plessey at Addlestone offered a software service to the public as well. It gave much-needed advice on computer installations and could supply Apple computers together with whatever software was needed, and provide full service (67).

An important part of the activity was instruction. Users of equipment, service officers and operators came from all over the world and took courses of instruction given by lecturers.

Navigational aids were developed, including direction-finders. Telecommunications were handled by another group, but remote data handling and transmission figured, and stabilised receiving dishes were developed, for use on ships in naval satellite communications. Flight recorders were developed and instrument landing systems for aircraft.

One group worked on environmental studies, surveys of earth resources, estimation of rainfall with the optimum location of reservoirs, measurement of water flow and river control.

Transmission by optical fibres was studied and developed, and heat sensors were designed which can be used in the location of those trapped or buried by collapses and earthquakes. Plessey Naval Systems worked on underwater systems and sonar equipment (61, 62, 63, 64, 65).

An airfield built by Plessey Airfields in Grenada was destroyed by the U. S. Marine Corps in the invasion of 1983. The field was re-built by Plessey. Plessey Services, a unit of Plessey Radar, provided resident servicing overseas. Jim Abra, of that unit, was imprisoned in Libya for "spying". Plessey ship-borne radar was used by both sides in the Falklands War in 1982. A Plessey three-dimensional radar (AR3D) was installed in Port Stanley after the war.

18. G.E.C./SIEMENS

For some time, a combine of Siemens and G.E.C. had been attempting a take-over which was not, at first, successful. However, trading in shares ceased in September 1989, which may mean that a controlling interest had been reached. On April 21, 1989, the Monopolies & Mergers Commission had already given conditional approval to the bid. The staff was not informed until April 1990, and from that date the Plessey building in Addlestone was re-named "Marconi".

19. PHASES OF ACTIVITY

Three distinct phases can be seen. The Blériot period seems to mark a time of the amateur. Blériot was, in fact, a highly professional man of his day, though in cars rather than aircraft. Aircraft were in the experimental stage, though under pressure of war. But, even for the time, the company was small. In the Weymann time it differed. As in the Blériot period, it was a time of transition. Personality was still important in the early years. Weymann was an engineering innovator, still showing the qualities of the amateur. After he disappeared from the story the company depended on the quite different qualities of three men. Without Izod, Homfray-Davies and Froggatt, it is difficult to imagine continued success. Co-operation between different companies became more common and developed with time. The Plessey period shows the big international company with hundreds of branches and connections all over the world, where personalities seem less important.

REFERENCES

1. Ordnance Survey Maps. Scale 2500:1. 1914, 1934, 1964.
2. The Diary of Susan Harms. Chertsey Museum. Paper No. 3. Mar. 1974. B. F. J. Pardoe.
3. Flypast. Dec. 1982. (Blériot and flight).
4. The Aeroplane. Aug. 12, 1936. (Blériot).
5. Motor Sport. Dec. 1963.
6. The Aeroplanes of the Royal Flying Corps (Military Wing). J. M. Bruce. Putnam, 1982.
7. Council Approvals Book. Runnymede Borough Council.
8. Correspondence with Mr. Andrews, Chief Executive, Runnymede Borough Council.
9. The Story of M-C-W Progress. Weymann. C.1948.
10. 'Olympic' Integral Bus. Leyland M-C-W. Undated.
11. Twenty-one Years of M-C-W Progress. 1953.
12. Silver Jubilee Booklet. Metropolitan-Cammell-Weymann. 1957.
13. Weymag. House Magazine. 1949 & Silver Jubilee, July 1950.
14. Luncheon Menus. Silver Jubilee of Weymann's. June 16 & 22, 1950.
15. Sports Programmes and Membership Card of Weymann's Sports & Social Club. July 11, 1953 & May 25, 1957.
16. Surrey Herald. July 7, 1961. (Fire).
17. Surrey Herald. Feb. 21 to July 31, 1964. (Strike).
18. Surrey Herald. June 25, 1965 to Feb. 4, 1966. (Closure).
19. Daily Telegraph. May 20, 1963. (United Molasses Company).
20. Surrey Herald. Jan. 13, 1967. (Conversion).
21. Basic Facts About the Move. Plessey Radar Booklet. Sept. 1966.
22. Kelly's Directories. 1913, 1915, 1918, 1919, 1922 & later.
23. Aeroplane Monthly. Sept. 1984, Jan. & June 1985.
24. Aeroplane Monthly. Jan. 1979.
25. Weymann's Schedule. 1939.
26. British Civil Aircraft since 1919. Vol. 1. A. J. Jackson. Putnam. 1974.
27. British Military Aircraft Serials 1911-1979. Bruce Robertson. Patrick Stephens. 1979.
28. British Aeroplanes 1914-1918. J. M. Bruce. Putnam. 1957.
29. National Motor Museum, Beaulieu.
30. The Golden Jubilee Souvenir. 1902-1952. L. W. Gray. Addlestone Co-op.
31. Brooklands. Brooklands Museum. 1985.
32. Flight. 1913.
33. Rate Books, 1906, 1914, 1926, 1932, 1934, 1935, 1944, etc. Chertsey Museum.
34. Lang. Mr. Goodall's file. Brooklands Museum. Aeronautics, June 23, 1915.
35. Elmbridge Museum.
36. Overseers of Chertsey Minute Book. 1915-24. Chertsey Museum.
37. Correspondence with Mr. N. Froggatt. Jan. 1988.
38. The Shuttleworth Collection.
39. Motor Specifications to 1930. Stone & Cox (Publications) Ltd.

40. Specification of chain-driven Blériot Whippet. Chertsey Museum.
41. Motor Show Handbooks. 1923/4. Society of Motor Manufacturers & Traders.
42. Brooklands Museum.
43. Correspondence. British Aerospace.
44. Rolland Jerry. Old Motor. P. 357 et seq., Vol. 1. 1962.
45. The Automobile. Aug. 1983. P. 48 et seq.
46. O. Heim. Veteran and Vintage Magazine. Jan/Feb. 1971. P. 164 et seq.
47. Montagu of Beaulieu & Georgano. Early Days on the Road. 1976.
48. Montagu of Beaulieu. The Gordon Bennett Races. 1963.
49. Bellu, S. et al. 100 Ans d'Automobile Francaise. P. 67. 1984.
50. Companies Registration Office. Weymann's Motor Bodies (1925) Ltd. No. 209936.
51. The Illustrated Encyclopaedia of Aircraft. Hamlyn. 1978.
52. Gordon Morrison, Librarian. I.Mech.E., 1, Birdcage Walk, Westminster, SW1H 9JJ.
53. The Complete Book of Automobile Body Design. Ian Beattie. Haynes. 1977.
54. Minutes of the National Union of Vehicle Builders. Chertsey Museum.
55. The Merits of Weymann Body Construction. The Commercial Motor. May 7, 1929. P. 432.
56. Flight. May 22, 1914. (Norbert Chéreau).
57. Shell Aviation News. No. 252. June, 1959.
58. Flight. 1909.
59. Plan of St. George's College, Weybridge.
60. Soundings. Dec. 1988. The house magazine of Plessey Naval Systems.
61. Plessey Electronics. Special Issue. 1969.
62. Systems Technology, No. 26. June 1977.
63. Systems Technology, No. 27. November 1977.
64. Plessey in Action. 1969/70.
65. Systems Technology. August 1970. (Air Traffic Control).
66. Plessey internal notices.
67. Plessey Information Engineering advertisement. 1988.
68. Letters from Norbert Chéreau to L. Blériot. Musée de l'Aérospace, Le Bourget.
69. Letter from L. Blériot to Minister of Finance. Musée de l'Aérospace, Le Bourget.
70. Notes on Charles Terres Weymann. Musée de l'Aérospace, Le Bourget.
71. V. Mitchell & K. Smith, "Branch Lines around Ascot". Middleton Press 1989.
72. Surrey Herald. June 1945.

INDEX